YANKEE AIR MUSEUM

Lt. Col. Richard Cole gives a thumbs-up to the B-25 *Yankee Warrior* at the 75th anniversary commemoration of the Doolittle Raid, held at the National Museum of the United States Air Force in Dayton, Ohio, in April 2017.

FRONT COVER: The B-17 *Yankee Lady* is the crown jewel of the Yankee Air Museum's fleet of aircraft. Museum volunteers spent nine years and countless hours restoring this aircraft. (Courtesy Yankee Air Museum/Roger Hart.)

UPPER BACK COVER: The 2014 Rosie the Riveter event featured 776 Rosies. (Courtesy of Al Hudson; see page 58.)

LOWER BACK COVER (FROM LEFT TO RIGHT): The C-47 *Yankee Doodle Dandy* is pictured in front of Hangar One at Willow Run airport (courtesy of Roger Hart; see pages 15 and 27), this UH-1D "Huey" helicopter is on display at the Yankee Air Museum (courtesy of Melissa Workman; see pages 37 and 44), the B-17 *Yankee Lady* comes in for a landing (courtesy of Yankee Air Museum; see page 11).

YANKEE AIR MUSEUM

Barry D. Levine

ARCADIA
PUBLISHING

Published by Arcadia Publishing
Charleston, South Carolina

Printed in the United States of America

Library of Congress Control Number: 2018949073

For all general information, please contact Arcadia Publishing:
Telephone 843-853-2070
Fax 843-853-0044
E-mail sales@arcadiapublishing.com
For customer service and orders:
Toll-Free 1-888-313-2665

Visit us on the Internet at www.arcadiapublishing.com

To the memory of
Sam Levine, US Army Air Force
Frank Quattro, US Marine Corps
Terry Quattro, US Marine Corps.

CONTENTS

ACKNOWLEDGMENTS

Writing this book was an absolute pleasure and would have been impossible without 100 percent backing from the leadership team of the Yankee Air Museum, including Dennis Norton, Randy Hotton, Ray Hunter, and Kevin Walsh.

Four other people—Julie Osborne (the Yankee Air Museum's curatorial director and a limitless source of information), Al Hudson and Dwight Koslowski (both of whom provided access and permission to choose from thousands of photographs), and Harry Terpstra (who shared extensive background information on the museum's founding) deserve special mention.

Additionally, in varied ways, these individuals and organizations made significant contributions: Alison Beatty, Dave Callanan, Bob Catalano, Chris Curran, Norm Ellickson, Megan Favio, Darlene Imus, Les Klima, Ralph Koehler, Jerry Lester, Mike Luther, John Marker, Ashley Myers, Heide Otto, Tony Pequeno, Kevin Perlongo, Dave Steiner, Bruce Stoddart, Cheryl Tumpkin, Barret Vance, Melissa Workman, John Yates, Belleville Area Museum, University of Michigan Bentley Historical Library, Ypsilanti Auto Heritage Museum, and Ypsilanti Historical Society.

Also, a very special thank-you to my children, Dan and Jessica, who supported and encouraged me from day one of this project, and my wife, Carole, who not only provided encouragement and support but professional-grade editing as well.

The following abbreviations are used throughout this book:

AFB	Air Force Base
EAA Fly-In	Experimental Aircraft Association Convention & Fly In
GM	General Motors
MAF	Michigan Aerospace Foundation
MIAT	Michigan Institute of Aviation and Technology
NMAT	National Museum of Aviation and Technology at Historic Willow Run
NMUSAF	National Museum of the United States Air Force
NNAM	National Naval Aviation Museum
RACER	Revitalizing Auto Communities Environmental Response Trust
Thunder	Thunder Over Michigan

INTRODUCTION

If you love aviation and history, this is the place to be.
—Chris Curran, Restoration

Why write a book about the Yankee Air Museum?

As it turns out, there is an extraordinary story behind the Yankee Air Museum, as well as its relationship with the Willow Run Airport and Bomber Plant. This book's goals are to acknowledge the tireless dedication of the volunteers who have preserved this history; highlight specific exhibits, events, and speakers; and discuss the museum's founding and future plans.

To really understand the museum's unique history, some background on the Willow Run complex is necessary.

One aspect is the Willow Run Airport, which was once Detroit's primary passenger airport and now handles cargo (over 200 million tons annually), commercial, and general aviation business. Willow Run gets very busy every summer when the museum hosts a popular and impressive air show, Thunder Over Michigan. Wayne County Airport Authority, which operates the airport, contributes substantial resources and support.

A second aspect is a 144,000-square-foot remnant of the Willow Run bomber plant, which was a key part of the Arsenal of Democracy during World War II. Over 8,600 Consolidated B-24 Liberator bombers were built in a 3.5-million-square-foot factory on the west side of the airport. Numerous published works cover the plant, including *Willow Run*, by Randy Hotton and Michael Davis, available from Arcadia Publishing.

The third aspect is today's Yankee Air Museum, where visitors find aircraft and unique artifacts filling 28,000 square feet of gallery space, with more aircraft outside. The museum, in a former Michigan Institute of Aviation and Technology (MIAT) training facility on Willow Run's east side, will move in the early 2020s to the Willow Run bomber plant remnant, which is being renovated into a state-of-the-art museum and event center. The new museum will be known as the National Museum of Aviation and Technology at Historic Willow Run (NMAT) and will include more aircraft, artifacts, and interactive exhibits showcasing American military aviation history and industrial might.

EARLY YEARS

The museum's origins go back to the summer of 1981, when two local aviation enthusiasts, Dennis Norton (the museum's first member) and the late Gary Bassett (the second member), began considering a B-24 project. As B-24s had been manufactured at Willow Run, why not bring a B-24 "back home" and set it up for display? The idea got a life of its own and became even better when they wondered, in a half-joking way, "Why not *fly* the B-24?"

This sort of effort would take people, time, and money. In the late summer of 1981, Norton and Bassett went to the Selfridge Air Force Base (AFB) air show and met with Selfridge Military Air Museum founder Bob Stone and Don O'Dell, an F-105 pilot who was shot down and captured by the North Vietnamese and later became the public affairs officer at Selfridge Air National Guard base. Norton and Bassett spent three days at Selfridge, generating a lot of ideas and getting things moving—the Selfridge people were very supportive of an aviation venture at Willow Run.

Later that year, a core group of enthusiasts including Norton, Bassett, Patti Meyer, Greg Smith, Cindy Smith, Bill Lary, Dennis Neveu, and Lee Koepke began discussing next steps. The first official museum meeting was on September 24, 1981. Next was placing an ad in the *Ann Arbor News* to solicit public participation. This resulted in the museum's first public meeting, in the basement of the Ann Arbor Airport Terminal, on October 8, 1981. November 1981 coverage in the *Ann Arbor News* noted an open house and a public meeting.

The hard work of making the museum a reality began with subsequent biweekly sessions (and in an era before e-mail and Facebook, countless phone calls). All sorts of questions needed to be addressed: What was the mission of the new organization? Where would new members come from? How would it be financed?

The organization also needed a name. Early on in 1981, Norton and Bassett were discussing the project in front of Butler Aviation, a private aviation firm at Willow Run. At that moment, a blue Air American Yankee aircraft with a star on the wheel taxied and parked in front of them. That was it! Norton suggested the museum be called Yankee Air Force (later evolving into Yankee Air Museum in the late 1980s and early 1990s). After the board voted, several members proposed that the museum become the Michigan wing of the Confederate Air Force—now the Commemorative Air Force—but the full board decided to remain an independent entity. A contest was held to create a logo; Harry Terpstra, a future president of the museum, submitted the winning design.

The museum also needed a home to begin operations. A surplus hangar, No. 2041, which was used to train B-24 support crews on the east side of Willow Run, became available. After a considerable amount of work to get the facility ready to open, the hangar was dedicated in May 1982.

An early organizational goal was to obtain a Willow Run–built B-24. This proved to be an insurmountable challenge, as there are only two flyable B-24s in the world, neither of which were built at the bomber plant. There are four Willow Run B-24s on static display, one in the United States, one in Canada, and two in the United Kingdom. The museum does have a Willow Run–built fuselage (see page 54).

The early museum had many other objectives: commemorate history, fly airplanes, build a museum, teach future generations about the story of Willow Run, meet and learn from museum visitors who have their own stories to tell, and build lasting friendships with great people.

This was a huge undertaking for an organization with scant resources. During the 1980s, the museum purchased three flyable aircraft: a B-17, a B-25, and a C-47. The board and volunteers remained steadfast and over time built a fleet of flyable and static aircraft, while undertaking numerous restoration projects. Each of the acquisitions has its own unique story, such as when nine members took out second mortgages on their homes to help finance the B-17's purchase in 1986. With each year, the collection expanded, bringing in more visitors and visibility.

2004 FIRE: RISING FROM THE ASHES

The museum's steady growth came to an abrupt stop when disaster struck on October 9, 2004. A devastating fire, the cause of which remains unknown, destroyed the hangar and much of the aircraft, as well as artifacts, equipment, tooling, and many of the organization's records.

Fortunately, quick-thinking volunteers on site during the blaze towed and pushed the flyable aircraft out of the burning hangar. Their bravery saved the flyables—and very likely the museum's future. At an emergency meeting the next day, members decided that the museum would rebuild. A hat was passed, and $184 was collected on the spot. In short order, word got out about the fire, and donations began coming in—ranging from the History Channel to supporters from countries such as Canada, Australia, and England.

News of the fire quickly spread in the aviation community. Mike Whaley of the OV-10 Bronco Association (one of the aircraft destroyed in the fire) said in reference to restoration efforts:

> While the loss of so much irreplaceable history at the museum is heartbreaking, we are encouraged to know that it's not as simple as "game over." The volunteers that keep a museum such as the Yankee Air Force going are a special breed of folks, who couldn't do what they do if they were easily deterred by adversity. These folks view "impossible" odds not as a deterrent, but as a challenge to be met with enthusiasm. We look forward to seeing the Yankee Air Museum rebuild from the ashes with an even bigger and better facility and collection.

Whaley was precisely right in describing the museum's approach and in predicting the future.

PRESENT

Since the fire, the museum has had several temporary homes, including its current location, which opened six years to the day after the fire in 2010. The small paid and large volunteer staff have rebuilt—and over time, expanded—exhibits and programming to include supporting and providing hundreds of volunteers for the annual Thunder Over Michigan air show; hosting various speakers and authors discussing aviation, military, and historic themes; honoring the role of women in World War II defense plants by supporting the Willow Run Tribute Rosies, who perform at numerous events throughout the year; engaging in a friendly competition with the Rosie the Riveter World War II Home Front Park in California for the Guinness World Record for the most Rosies gathered in one spot at one time; providing science, history, and aviation programming for youth; restoring vintage aircraft; and offering rides on flyable aircraft to the public.

During this rebuilding phase, the museum moved from a member-based organization with annual election of the board by the entire membership to a director-based organization with appointed directors who provide specialized knowledge, skills, and perspectives. These organizational changes allow the board to take a longer view and act on the museum's strategic needs.

The museum continues moving forward with new traveling exhibits and aircraft acquisitions. Three of the most recent aircraft added to the inventory include a Lockheed Neptune P2V-7, a Bell AH-1J Sea Cobra, and a Douglas SBD Dauntless acquired from the National Naval Aviation Museum (NNAM). The Dauntless had crashed into Lake Michigan in a 1943 training flight and will be displayed upside down—as it was found at the bottom of the lake. The exhibit will be known as Deep Landings.

THUNDER OVER MICHIGAN

The annual air show Thunder Over Michigan has its own impressive history. While various air shows had been held at Willow Run over the years, Thunder had its roots in 1999. An 18-year-old museum member, Michael Luther, suggested a combination of a symposium and an air show—inviting World War II veterans for a dinner and discussion along with flying in and displaying aircraft.

Inclement weather resulted in only two P-51 Mustangs flying in for the 1999 Mustang Round-Up and Symposium. Speakers included Robert Morgan (B-17 *Memphis Belle* pilot), Clarence "Bud" Anderson (World War II triple-ace fighter pilot), and Gunther Rall (World War II Luftwaffe pilot). The speakers were well received, but it was not obvious from this small beginning that Thunder would become one of the premier air shows in the United States.

A very partial list of Thunder highlights over the years includes:

2003   First use of the Thunder name.
2004   World-record World War II Avenger torpedo bomber gathering.
2005   Show went on despite the 2004 fire.
        Eight B-17s attended—a record that has been equaled but never surpassed.
2007   First Blue Angels appearance; world record B-25 gathering.
2009   Board authorized the 2009 show by one vote. It became the most profitable to date despite a weak Michigan economy and the risk of financial losses.
2011   Hosted Centennial of Naval Aviation, one of 32 locations in the United States.
2013   Overcame the challenges of the federal government's sequestration to put on a very successful Thunder.
2014   First appearance of the Air Force Thunderbirds.
2017   Reenactment of World War II paratroop drop; largest paratroop reenactment in the world.

FUTURE

The current facility is too small to be the museum's permanent home. After World War II, the Willow Run bomber plant was sold to Kaiser-Frazer, which built cars, tractors, and a small number of airplanes. The plant was then purchased by General Motors (GM), primarily for building automobile transmissions.

As part of the ongoing effort to find space for the museum's aircraft after the fire, Dennis Norton called Bob Lutz, then a senior GM executive. The original idea was to store the B-17 *Yankee Lady* in the rollout hangar where B-24s came off the Willow Run line. GM, however, was having financial difficulties and closed the entire facility in 2010. The plant was sold to the Revitalizing Auto Communities Environmental Response (RACER) Trust, an organization managing GM's real estate holdings. RACER tried to sell the entire facility, but there were no takers.

After extended negotiations, the museum purchased 144,000 square feet of the original plant in 2014; the remainder has since been torn down. RACER set a fundraising goal of $8 million—a relatively small amount of $144,000 to purchase the plant, with the remainder sufficient to begin rebuilding the structure. Despite extending the deadline several times, by May 2014, funds raised were short of the $8 million target. What put the museum over the top, however, was an *NBC Nightly News* feature that spurred additional interest and more donations. The sale was completed in late 2014.

Significant resources are needed to renovate a World War II–era factory; although it would have been easier to build a new facility on the airport grounds, the history within this building makes it the perfect setting to honor the nation's aviation past.

The site is steadily being transformed, including power-washing and painting the exterior, repairing the structure, and removing debris and scrap materials. An extensive drainage system has been installed to clear groundwater underneath the site (RACER manages environmental remediation efforts). During the next several years, contractors will install electrical infrastructure, fire suppression, potable water, sanitary sewer, and concrete flooring.

The support of individual donors and corporate gifts are making this all possible, with local businesses and labor unions contributing substantial in-kind donations of material, equipment, and skilled workers. The museum plans to begin moving into the new facility in the early 2020s, likely in several phases. At that time, the name Yankee Air Museum will be retired and replaced with National Museum of Aviation and Technology at Historic Willow Run.

THE VOLUNTEER AIR FORCE

It is not an overstatement to say that the museum would not exist without volunteers. Since its founding, thousands of people have given countless hours of their time, along with expertise and energy, to ensure the quality visitors have come to appreciate.

There is a limitless supply of history on hand, and the museum's team help tell the story—sometimes from a personal perspective. For example, John Marker has been on the restoration team for years, machining and fabricating parts for the Consolidated PB4Y-2 Privateer, a Navy derivative of the B-24. Marker's father was a B-24 gunner in World War II, so working on the Privateer was a natural for him.

Once, part of the PB4Y-2's outer wing had to be removed to replace corroded aluminum skin and stringers. This required removing over 160 corroded bolts without any convenient access. Restoration volunteers crawled up through a wheel well to get at them. This work was done in a hot, un–air conditioned hangar with virtually no room to work—the crew hammered, chiseled, punched, sawed, and mainly cussed to get them out. Finally, they removed all the corroded bolts, repairing what they could and remaking others, replacing them all. "To put it bluntly," Marker said, "it was a pain, and I loved—and hated—every minute of it."

Why would John Marker and all his fellow volunteers do this? For friendship, camaraderie, and more. Much more. "We come every week to preserve our heritage," he says, "and what our fathers went through in the war."

One

THE EARLY DAYS

This hangar was the museum's first home, which was lost in the 2004 fire. The B-17 *Yankee Lady* is in front. This 1941 structure, known at the time as the Ford Airplane School, was used to train B-24 ground crews during World War II. Museum founder Dennis Norton made a presentation to the Wayne County Road Commission in January 1982 requesting use of this hangar, expecting a counter offer of a smaller facility. Instead, the commission's decision was "you've got it." (Courtesy of Dwight Koslowski.)

In former president Harry Terpstra's view, volunteers had "nothing but the love of aviation, a dream of starting a museum and bringing a Ford-built B-24 back to Willow Run." That love would be tested—volunteers spent hours chipping off frozen floor tiles in an unheated hangar that first winter. At least one case of frostbite was reported; extensive rehabilitation work to the entire structure was required. (Courtesy of Dennis Norton.)

Mike Bergeron, Brian Conley, and Dick Kolbas formed a hangar committee to coordinate the renovation. Personnel from the nearby GM transmission plant provided considerable expertise. The museum was publicly dedicated on May 16, 1982, four and a half months after its acquisition. The aircraft on the right in front of the hangar is a Douglas A-1 Skyraider; also shown is the Douglas C-47 that became the *Yankee Doodle Dandy* and later, *Hairless Joe*. (Courtesy of Dennis Norton.)

Dedication day also featured *Gallant Warrior,* a North American B-25 Mitchell that was owned by World War II veteran and B-25 collector Glenn Lamont. This B-25 was later purchased by Yankee and renamed *Yankee Warrior.* Numerous dignitaries from the Michigan Aeronautics Commission, Wayne County, the Ypsilanti Visitors Bureau, and Ford Motor Company attended the ceremony. F-4 Phantoms from Selfridge Air National Guard base did a low, close-by flyover; vibrations from their engines caused "snow" paint chips to fall from the rafters. Having a facility ready for a public dedication was an amazing accomplishment for an organization less than a year old, with only 206 members, and $4,272 in the bank at the end of 1981—highlighting what a group of dedicated volunteers can accomplish. (Above, courtesy of Dennis Norton; below, courtesy of the Terpstra collection.)

The museum's first public meeting was held in October 1981 in the basement of the Ann Arbor Airport terminal. Attendees elected the first board. From left to right are (first row) Greg Smith, Harry Terpstra, Phil Lundy, Tom Wilkins, and Elmer Spencer; (second row) Patti Meyer, George Taylor, Dennis Norton, and Cindy Smith. Board members dealt with the many challenges of a start-up organization. (Courtesy of Dennis Norton.)

The 1985 board of directors included, from left to right, (first row) Todd Hackbarth, Barbara Sutton, Louise Greenwald, Nancy Lockwood, Patti Meyer, Dennis Norton, Harry Terpstra, and Ralph Gilpin; (second row) Larry Silver, Bill Wier, Frank Modlinski, Audrey Ray, and Al Bittner. There are about 1,500,000 US nonprofit organizations; all deal with a very competitive market for donations of time, funds, and support. (Courtesy of Dennis Norton.)

Bob Hoover was one of the great aviators in US history. He saw World War II combat, was a military test pilot (he flew the chase plane when Chuck Yeager broke the sound barrier in 1947), then spent years in civilian aviation in a wide range of test and air-show pilot roles. Jimmy Doolittle called Hoover the greatest stick-and-rudder pilot of all time. This photograph shows Hoover (left) and Dennis Norton in 1982. (Courtesy of Dennis Norton.)

The Douglas C-47 *Yankee Doodle Dandy* won the Best Transport category at the 1985 EAA Fly-In in Oshkosh, Wisconsin—one of the world's largest air shows. The award recognized the hardworking museum team that keeps the C-47 and other flyable aircraft in the air. *Yankee Doodle Dandy* made a cameo appearance in the 1992 HBO film *Citizen Cohn*. (Courtesy of Dwight Koslowski.)

The Michigan Aeronautics Commission oversees aviation related matters as part of Michigan's Department of Transportation. In 2003, the museum received the Award of Excellence. Accepting the award were Dennis Norton (second from left), Frank Sinagra (third from left, now on the board of the Michigan Aerospace Foundation), and Jon Stevens (fourth from left, former president of the museum). (Courtesy of Yankee Air Museum.)

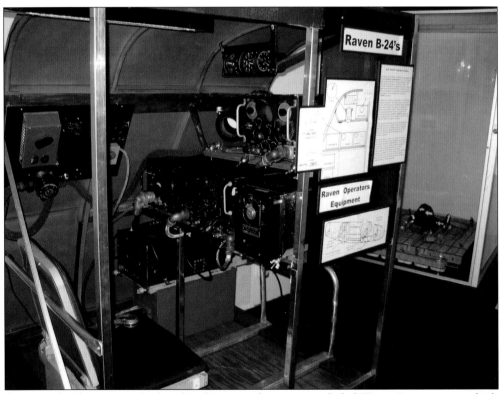

An example of rare items displayed at the original museum included "Raven" equipment, which had its origins with British development of radar before World War II. American and British scientists and military personnel continued developing radar and radar countermeasures throughout the war, searching for technological advancements to fight the Axis. Various aircraft, including certain B-24s, were equipped with this technology. (Courtesy of Dwight Koslowski.)

The museum had an extraordinary collection of artifacts that were mostly lost in the fire—uniforms, artwork, flight instruments, photographs, books—even a Japanese samurai sword. A conservation laboratory was established for any salvageable items. Thanks to the generosity of the membership and the local community, the artifact collection was rebuilt; many outstanding items are now on display and more will be shown at NMAT. (Courtesy of Dwight Koslowski.)

This is the original hangar's interior, with some of the aircraft on hand. At bottom left is a Republic F-105 Thunderchief that was undergoing restoration. This F-105 flew with the Air Force Thunderbirds in 1963–1964 and served at a number of US bases. It was delivered in 1996 from the National Museum of the United States Air Force (NMUSAF) and was in the final stages of restoration when the fire occurred. (Courtesy of Dwight Koslowski.)

Pictured is the first aircraft obtained by the museum, a Republic RF-84K Thunderflash, which was displayed in a park in Belleville, Michigan. After discussions with Belleville officials, the RF-84K, which was on loan from NMUSAF, was "given" to the museum, whose volunteers restored it. NMUSAF requested and received the return of this aircraft. A second RF-84, now on display, was then obtained. (Courtesy of Dwight Koslowski.)

This North American Rockwell Y-OV-10A Bronco was destroyed in the fire; it had been used by NASA to test low-speed flying characteristics. Richard Rice led a nine-year restoration effort. After the fire, Rice commented to the OV-10 Association: "I'm so sorry for all the Nam vets that had anything to do with the Bronco; I spent nine years restoring her . . . to make a memorial to all you guys." (Courtesy of Dwight Koslowski.)

The Cessna L-19 Bird Dog (later O-1) was used as a military observation aircraft in both Korea and Vietnam; it was based on Cessna's civilian 305 aircraft. L-19s were used on Forward Air Control missions to target enemy positions. This aircraft is pictured at Willow Run during a 2004 Vietnam commemoration event sponsored by the Vietnam Veterans of America Plymouth/ Canton chapter. (Courtesy of Dwight Koslowski.)

Shown is a Weaver Aircraft Company of Ohio (WACO) CG-4A glider that was lost in the fire. CG-4As were a workhorse during World War II, participating in Allied landings at Normandy, Sicily, and various combat zones in Asia. Also pictured is longtime restoration volunteer Joe Kosek, a World War II glider pilot who saw action in Burma and New Guinea. (Courtesy of Yankee Air Museum.)

A Curtiss P-40 Warhawk is pictured at Thunder 2003 in front of the original hangar. This aircraft was delivered to the Royal Canadian Air Force in 1941. After several ownership changes, it returned to flying status as *Old Exterminator*, in honor of the P-40 flown by the late Gen. Robert Scott with the "Flying Tigers" in China. (Courtesy of Dwight Koslowski.)

Aviation legend Chuck Yeager is pictured at Thunder 2003. Yeager is one of the all-time great aviators. He flew in World War II, Korea, and Vietnam. As a test pilot, he broke the sound barrier in a Bell X-1 in 1947. Yeager has flown many aircraft associated with the museum, such as the F-86, F-100, F-4, and the B-57. (Courtesy of Dwight Koslowski.)

Two

THE FLYABLE AIRCRAFT

Legend has it that the Boeing B-17 got its name, "Flying Fortress," from a journalist seeing multiple machine guns on a prototype's flight. B-17s, along with B-24s, were heavy bombers used in the air assault on the Axis during World War II. The museum purchased this former Coast Guard B-17 in 1986 for $250,000. The subsequent years of restoration work resulted in this beautiful aviation icon. (Courtesy of Dwight Koslowski.)

The Coast Guard used B-17s until 1959. The museum's aircraft would have looked similar to the one pictured here in her Coast Guard days. These B-17s were deployed with a lifeboat/parachute slung under the fuselage to be dropped to survivors on search and rescue missions. Restoration work included converting the Coast Guard configuration to the original World War II design. (Courtesy of Yankee Air Museum.)

This photograph was taken on the B-17's arrival from Arizona in July 1986. On the far right is pilot Dick Bodycombe, who had a distinguished military career—he was a World War II B-24 and Berlin airlift pilot, and an early faculty member at the Air Force Academy. Glenn Lamont, previous owner of the *Yankee Warrior*, is wearing the light shirt and blue baseball cap on the left. (Courtesy of the Terpstra collection.)

Restoration of the *Yankee Lady* is seen here. The project took nine years to complete, involving the work of over 300 volunteers. Restoration work on vintage aircraft is very specialized and labor intensive; volunteers work off of old blueprints. Parts are difficult to find, can be expensive, or may have to be custom made with specialized tooling. Norm Ellickson, the B-17 crew chief, participates in a network with other B-17 owners to facilitate trading for parts. Ellickson is recognized in the B-17 world as the "go-to guy" for B-17 mechanical questions and led *Yankee Lady*'s restoration effort. In his words, "We'll keep her flying as long as humanly possible. Our veterans deserve nothing less." (Both, courtesy of Yankee Air Museum.)

Work on the B-17 was assisted by purchasing 26 rolls of microfilmed blueprints from the Smithsonian Institution. The museum team translated the prints into action, as shown in this photograph of two volunteers installing Cleco fasteners to hold sheet metal together as part of the riveting work. As of 2017, *Yankee Lady* had about 9,800 hours of flight time recorded—equivalent to more than one million air miles. (Courtesy of Yankee Air Museum.)

Nine years of effort paid off on July 13, 1995—with the first flight of the restored *Yankee Lady*—crewed by Bill Dodds, Dick Bodycombe, Fred Lockwood, Norm Ellickson, and two FAA employees. *Yankee Lady* began regularly participating in air shows; in the words of chief mechanic Paul Hakala, "When . . . we see a World War II B-17 veteran reunite with this airplane, the point of our freedom is driven home." (Courtesy of Yankee Air Museum.)

24

Some restoration projects became work-at-home initiatives. Volunteer Barret Vance worked on the *Yankee Lady's* chin and top turret in his garage. The *Yankee Lady's* ball turret (pictured) was used on the set of the 1990 movie *Memphis Belle* and was then purchased by the museum. The multiple pieces were rebuilt and restored by Norm Ellickson, working in his garage. (Courtesy of Dwight Koslowski.)

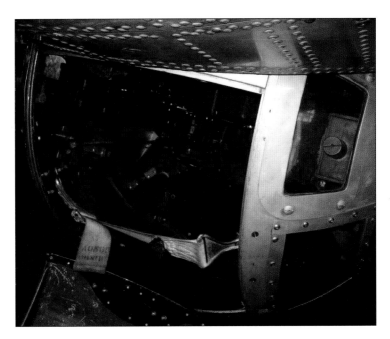

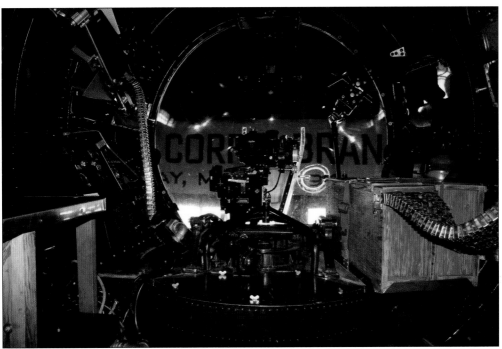

The World War II bombardier's primary tool was the Norden bombsight, seen here in the *Yankee Lady's* nose. A bombardier's duties are described on the 303rd Bomb Group's website: "Effective bombing is the ultimate purpose of your entire airplane and crew. . . . When the bombardier takes over the airplane for the [target] run, he is in absolute command . . . until he tells you 'Bombs away,' his word is law." (Courtesy of Al Hudson.)

Yankee Lady is finished in the livery of the 381st Bomb Group, 8th Air Force, based in Ridgewell, England. Joseph Slavik was a major donor in acquiring this aircraft and was a pilot in the 381st, flying 35 missions. The nose art is representative of the era; the art might reflect a crewman's hometown, girlfriend, or a favorite pin-up girl of the era. (Courtesy of Yankee Air Museum.)

One of the museum's missions is to promote interest in aviation history, particularly in youth. What better way than to take a group of students on a ride in the *Yankee Lady* and let their imagination wander? Reading about World War II bombers is one thing, but flying in one is something else altogether. This 2013 photograph shows the *Yankee Lady* and a high school group from Caledonia, Michigan. (Courtesy of Al Hudson.)

The C-47 *Yankee Doodle Dandy* was the museum's first flyable aircraft, purchased from Environmental Research Institute of Michigan (ERIM) in 1982. Museum personnel conducted a worldwide search for a B-24. Aircraft in India, Mexico, and Bolivia were considered. The B-24 search was unsuccessful, but this C-47 became available and was purchased. ERIM provided very favorable pricing, financing, and spare parts. (Photograph by Roger Hart.)

Volunteers Ron Haviland and Fred Lockwood led the effort to restore the C-47, taking 18 months. It was well worth the effort; passengers may consider the C-47's distinguished history during their flights. Known as the "Gooney Bird," the C-47 saw service in World War II, the Berlin Airlift, Korea, and Vietnam. C-47s towed gliders, transported cargo, dropped paratroops, and served as gun platforms. (Courtesy of Al Hudson.)

Museum flyables have been demonstrated at various air shows for years. This scene is from the 2014 Train Expo at Owosso, Michigan (which included aircraft as well as trains), and shows the museum's C-47 and B-25, as well as a P-51 Mustang. Participation in air shows allows the museum to bring living history to various parts of the country, as well as promoting the museum's work. (Courtesy of Al Hudson.)

Shown are satisfied passengers after a 2014 ride on the C-47. The museum successfully experimented with a shorter, less costly trip to expand ridership in 2017—a 20-minute takeoff and ride around Willow Run called Fly the Pattern. Longer rides in the area have covered southeast Michigan highlights, such as the University of Michigan football stadium. In mid-2018, the C-47 was repainted and renamed *Hairless Joe* in honor of one of its pilots, who supposedly looked like the character from the *Li'l Abner* comic. (Courtesy of Al Hudson.)

In 1987, the museum welcomed three Tuskegee Airmen from the Detroit chapter. They are pictured here wearing blue blazers in front of the B-25 *Gallant Warrior*. In addition to its eight combat missions in World War II from Corsica, this aircraft was used by the Royal Canadian Air Force in various training roles. The museum obtained it in 1987; restoration work began in 2000, with the first flight in July 2003. (Courtesy of the Terpstra collection.)

One step in achieving FAA certification is completion of an emergency evacuation within 90 seconds. In May 1993, a group of 10 museum members tested the process and successfully evacuated in 34 seconds. Ultimately, rides were offered to the public; passengers on a 2008 flight saw this view of Detroit. At bottom left is Cobo Arena (former home of the Detroit Pistons). At bottom right is the Renaissance Center (home of General Motors' corporate offices). (Courtesy of Chris Curran.)

Restoration volunteers assessed the condition of the B-17; it was flyable, but in rough condition. The decision was made to completely overhaul the aircraft, a project that was originally estimated to take five or six years. The reality was that it was a nine-year effort, resulting in an aircraft that provides thrilling rides to its passengers, closely matches original specifications, and became an award winner at the EAA Fly-In. (Courtesy of Dwight Koslowski.)

A 2014 addition to the flyable aircraft fleet was a WACO YMF-5C. The Waco can carry two passengers and a pilot and was acquired to give visitors a sense of the pre–World War II barnstorming era. This modern aircraft, built in Battle Creek, Michigan, is modeled after the original WACO YMF-5C designed in the 1930s. Enhancements include adding modern instrumentation and improving passenger safety and comfort. (Courtesy of Al Hudson.)

Three

THE FIRE AND
THE AFTERMATH

As in the past, today's museum strives to provide guests a fun, safe, and educational experience on every visit. Volunteers in retail, security, and education departments strive to provide an excellent experience to every guest. Guests return the favor by sharing their own experiences. This photograph shows docent Terry Gunnell leading a tour. (Photograph by the author.)

On October 9, 2004, a fire broke out on the second floor; heroic efforts by volunteers on site saved the flyable aircraft. Volunteers such as Ken Chio, Tony Hurst, Lew Major Jr., Mary Jane Medlock, Bob Paul, Alan Running, and Ellie Staeger pushed and towed the B-25, B-17, and C-47 out of the burning hangar. Barret Vance had left a tow bar on the B-17 from his day's work, which was a huge help. Other than smoke inhalation, no one was injured, but the static aircraft, artifacts, organizational records, and equipment/tooling were largely destroyed. Many financial and computer records had off-site backup, helping the recovery. The cause of the fire was never determined with certainty. A small number of personnel remained that evening after the fire burned out. It is difficult to imagine what they were thinking, particularly since many of them had donated countless hours of work. (Both, courtesy of Ypsilanti Historical Society.)

Word went out the night of the fire to attend a meeting the next morning to figure out what to do next. On October 10, 2004, about 200 people attended the meeting, which was coincidentally held in the same building that became the museum's temporary home in 2010. The future had many challenges, but the decision was made to keep going and rebuild. The flyable and Air Park aircraft were not damaged, preserving the nucleus of the museum. Assistance for space and telephones was provided by Willow Run Airport and the Michigan Institute of Aeronautics. Meeting participants stepped outside and saw the B-25 flyover (the aerial photograph above was taken from the B-25). By all accounts, it was an emotional moment. The ground-level shot below with the B-52 in the foreground provides another perspective of the destruction. (Above, courtesy of Yankee Air Museum; below, courtesy of Dwight Koslowski.)

After World War II, Willow Run Airport, including the hangars, was sold to the University of Michigan at a price of $1. The complex was used for research purposes and as Detroit's airline terminal. The airport and hangar were transferred to Wayne County in 1977; in 2002, the Wayne County Airport Authority was created to oversee operations. After the fire destroyed the original museum in 2004, Yankee needed a facility for aircraft storage and offices. As one of the interim solutions, the museum was allowed to use space in Willow Run's Hangar 2. Given the poor condition of this facility, this was not a feasible long-term solution. These photographs of Hangar 2's interior show the Antonov AN-2 mid-restoration (above) and the *Yankee Warrior* with engine work underway below. (Both, courtesy of Dwight Koslowski.)

Extensive planning discussions with contractors and Willow Run Airport staff were held. One result was an April 2007 ground breaking for a new museum. Ultimately, the opportunity to save a portion of the bomber plant emerged and new plans were developed. Pictured are Tom Wilkins (a former vice president) and Harry Terpstra (former president and current board member of the Michigan Aerospace Foundation). (Courtesy of the Terpstra collection.)

The David and Andrea Robertson Education Center opened in 2010. The original building, which opened in 1938, was a school for boys working at Henry Ford's Camp Willow Run before the bomber plant and then as an officer's club. Charles Lindbergh slept in the building on some of his trips to Willow Run. The center has been renovated and serves as the museum's current research library. (Photograph by the author.)

In 2009, the museum purchased a building from MIAT that was previously used for training aviation technology students. These photographs show the current exterior of the facility, plus renovation work in 2009–2010 to convert the building to today's museum. The building is about 47,000 square feet, 28,000 of which house the museum gallery containing displays of aircraft and artifacts, with the remainder used for offices, storage, workshops, a gift shop, a movie theater, and a lecture hall. Special events, educational programs, and private parties are also held at the facility. When the bomber plant renovation is complete, this facility may be sold. (Above, photograph by the author; below, photograph by Al Hudson.)

Once the MIAT building was occupied, the museum needed to fill it with aircraft and artifacts. Shown is the move-in of the Bell UH-1 Iroquois "Huey" helicopter in 2010. This Huey saw service in Vietnam with various units, such as the 201st Aviation Company. It was shot down in 1967, written off as lost, and subsequently rebuilt. Since 2010, substantial restoration work on this helicopter has been completed. (Courtesy of Al Hudson.)

Guests can enjoy viewing an extensive collection of aviation-themed art in the art gallery, which opened in August 2017. On display are some of the works of aviation artist Ron Hart, who had a varied career—both as an American Airlines pilot (retiring in 2000) and as an artist. Hart spent free time from his airline travels studying works of art in museums worldwide to perfect his craft. (Photograph by the author.)

The post-fire recovery is highlighted in these photographs, one of which shows an open house in the new facility, a former MIAT building, in 2010. Opening day was six years to the day after the fire. The collection of aircraft and artifacts was very limited at move-in and has grown substantially in the following years. The photograph below shows the first general meeting of the membership in 2010 in the current location. General membership meetings were held on the first Wednesday of the month, now Historic Presentation Nights. The membership meeting below was hosted by interim executive director Randy Hotton (now on the board of directors). Kevin Walsh was appointed executive director in April 2012. Ray Hunter is presently chairman of the board. (Both, courtesy of Al Hudson.)

Four

Aircraft and Exhibits

This Douglas A-4C Skyhawk was obtained in 2016. The museum's aircraft was finished in the VA-216 livery by members of the Virginia Air National Guard and Naval Air Station Oceana in Virginia to honor Paul Galanti, an A-4C pilot and Vietnam prisoner of war (VA-216 was a naval attack squadron nicknamed the "Black Diamonds"). A-4s were designed by Douglas Aircraft's Ed Heinemann and were nicknamed "Heinemann's Hot Rod." (Courtesy of Melissa Workman.)

The McDonnell Douglas F-4 Phantom II saw service in the Air Force, Navy, and Marines from the 1960s to the 1990s. The museum's F-4C saw service in Vietnam with the 366th Tactical Fighter Wing, based in Da Nang. The finish on the aircraft honors pilot Lt. Loren Torkelson and weapons systems officer Lt. George Pollin, who were in the 366th. On an April 1967 mission, there was an on-board explosion, likely caused by enemy antiaircraft fire, resulting in the downing of their aircraft. Torkelson was captured by the North Vietnamese and Pollin died in the crash. Torkelson received a Silver Star for his actions that day; Pollin's body was returned home in 1990 and is buried in Arlington National Cemetery. (Both, courtesy of Melissa Workman.)

Cessna O-2 Skymaster missions in Vietnam included forward air control, reconnaissance, psychological operations, and CIA-related work. Detailed records of the museum's O-2, which saw service in Vietnam, are limited. This aircraft was found abandoned at Detroit's Metro Airport and was towed to Yankee in 2013—a three-hour job that began around 4:00 a.m., involving museum and airport personnel, with local law enforcement coordinating traffic. (Courtesy of Melissa Workman.)

Franklin PS-2 gliders were used during the 1930s as part of naval flight training. PS-2s were manufactured in Ypsilanti, Michigan, at 800 Railroad Street (a now-abandoned factory) and were designed by University of Michigan professor R.E. Franklin. The museum's glider, on permanent loan from the National Soaring Museum in Elmira, New York, was flown to the 1933 National Soaring Championship. (Photograph by the author.)

The EC-121 is the military variant of the Lockheed Constellation. EC-121s had a long career in military service. During the Vietnam War, they monitored sensors dropped on the Ho Chi Minh trail, listening for signs of enemy movements. In 2016, the Warning Star Rescue Project was launched to save an EC-121K, the museum's first aircraft loaned from the Navy. This particular aircraft was assigned to the Pacific Missile Test Center in Port Mugu, California, as a downrange missile tracker. The museum coordinated the disassembly, transport, and reassembly of this aircraft, which was unveiled at Thunder 2017. The photograph above showing the aircraft without propellers was taken at Chanute Aerospace Museum during disassembly. The fully assembled aircraft is seen below at Willow Run. (Above, photograph by Gary DeLisle; below, photograph by Al Hudson.)

The Republic RF-84F is a photo-reconnaissance aircraft. Yankee's RF-84F saw Air Force service and then became the last operational RF-84F in service with Michigan's Air National Guard. This aircraft was then displayed off of I-94 by Master Craft Industries in agreement with the Veterans of Foreign Wars Post 4434 in Belleville, Michigan. It was then loaned from the NMUSAF to the museum in 1988. (Courtesy of Roger Hart.)

This North American F-100C Super Sabre on loan from the NMUASF was obtained in part because it was the first Air Force fighter capable of supersonic speed in level flight. This particular aircraft was used for training mechanics at Amarillo AFB. F-100s were the first US supersonic fighters and flew more sorties than any other aircraft in Vietnam, primarily as a tactical fighter. (Photograph by the author.)

Aircraft in the Air Park were not damaged in the fire, such as this North American F-86D (later upgraded to an "L") Sabre. This F-86 had been displayed at General Electric's plant in Evendale, Ohio. It was acquired by William Hogan, an Ohio-based aviation enthusiast, who donated the aircraft to the museum in 1982. Elmer Spencer led the acquisition negotiations, and transport to Michigan was coordinated by Scott Vetter. (Photograph by the author.)

Huey helicopters were everywhere in Vietnam—troop insertion and extraction, medical evacuations, ferrying in supplies, reconnaissance, and forward air control. About 7,000 Hueys saw service in Vietnam, and about 3,300 were lost either to enemy action or mechanical function. Guests who served in Vietnam sometimes linger by the Huey. There are a lot of memories—some good, some bad, and some tragic—relating to this aircraft. (Courtesy of Melissa Workman.)

This de Havilland Canada DHC-4 is the oldest Caribou in existence. This Caribou was used briefly by Air America, the CIA's air operation, in the mid-1970s—some reference material indicates usage for training "smoke-jumpers"—who might later parachute into high-risk operations in Southeast Asia. This aircraft was obtained by the Environmental Research Institute of Michigan before its acquisition by the museum. (Courtesy of Al Hudson.)

Capt. Walter Batty served in the 20th Air Force in the Pacific. His family donated his uniform and many artifacts to the museum. Spiritual counsel provided by chaplains of all faiths was very important. US Marine Corps general Alexander Vandegrift said on October 23, 1945, "The ministrations you have carried to our fighting men have been an epic of spiritual heroism . . . You have gone wherever they have gone . . . You were helpers, advisers, listeners, and comforters." (Photograph by the author.)

Oral histories, as told by World War II veterans, have been recorded and are played in the exhibit theater pictured here. These veterans represent all military branches; there is no substitute for hearing directly from those who were there about their experiences. These interviews are part of the Library of Congress Veteran's History Project. Funding was provided by Ford Motor Company. (Photograph by the author.)

As part of the museum's mission to increase aviation knowledge in young people, the exhibit Five Simple Machines in Aviation (the basis of how aircraft fly) was opened in 2015. Seen here is a lever. Funding was provided by the General Motors Foundation and Wolf Aviation Fund. Volunteer Le Phan developed the design, assisted by the exhibits department and Rowe Thomas Display. (Photograph by the author.)

Charles McGee was one of the Tuskegee Airmen flying in the 332nd Fighter Group. The 332nd was very highly regarded and often requested by bomber units (crewed exclusively by white airmen) to provide escort. McGee flew 409 combat missions in World War II, Korea, and Vietnam. This was the emblem of McGee's 302nd squadron. (Photograph by the author.)

The R-4360 Pratt &Whitney engine is one of the largest piston engines ever built—approximate specifications are 3,500 pounds of weight and 3,000 horsepower. It has 28 cylinders arranged in seven banks of four cylinders each. R-4360s were also used in Howard Hughes's "Spruce Goose"—the largest airplane ever built. This engine was originally designed for the Goodyear F2G "Super" Corsair. (Photograph by the author.)

Chapter 310 of the Vietnam Veterans of America in Ann Arbor, Michigan, provided a great deal of assistance in constructing a Vietnam-era exhibit. Once completed, the vets signed the sandbags (including information such as name, rank, date of service, and location) as a reminder of who did the work. Since then, any Vietnam vet is welcome to sign, and hundreds have done just that. (Photograph by the author.)

Martin manufactured turrets for US and Allied World War II aircraft, such as the B-24. This turret was deployed on an Avro Lancaster X heavy bomber, built in Canada. The Canadians installed the American-made Martin turrets instead of British equipment, presumably because they were easier and cheaper to obtain. Turrets had an interrupter gear so the gunner could not shoot off his aircraft's tail. (Photograph by the author.)

Five

RESTORATION

A very long-term restoration project is the Consolidated PB4Y-2, pictured in 2012 as work progresses. Built in 1945 at Consolidated's plant in San Diego, California, the PB4Y-2 is the Navy derivation of the B-24. This particular aircraft served as a trainer and in weather reconnaissance for the Navy, then was configured for search and rescue work by the Coast Guard in 1952. (Courtesy of John Marker.)

After Coast Guard service, the PB4Y-2 was owned by a number of commercial enterprises from the 1950s to the 1970s. In 1975, flying on only one engine, the aircraft crash landed at Port Hardy, British Columbia, and was badly damaged. It slid off the runway, through a fence, and into a saltwater bay (the crew was not injured). The museum acquired this aircraft in 1986 as a gift from an anonymous donor. The restoration crew, headed by George Whitfield, had a monumental task to repair the crash damage and rebuild the plane, which had been cut into transportable-sized parts. Shown is the damaged fuselage upon its 1987 arrival; working inside the wing is restoration volunteer John Marker. This was not a good job for claustrophobes. (Above, courtesy of Dennis Norton; below, courtesy of John Marker.)

A Boeing B-52D Stratofortress is on display in the Air Park. This aircraft flew over 600 missions in Vietnam, including Operation Linebacker, which helped conclude the Vietnam conflict. It was flown to Yankee in 1983. A non-flyable B-52B (which had flown around the world without landing) was previously offered, but there was no feasible way to disassemble and transport it to Willow Run. Since the acquisition, the B-52's condition has deteriorated; extensive restoration work is underway involving the museum, MIAT, and the veterans who served at U-Tapao Royal Thai Navy Base in Thailand. Corroded engine cowlings that are being repaired are shown below. MIAT students have noted, "It's not every day you get to work on a piece of history." (Above, photograph by Dwight Koslowski; below, photograph by the author.)

Restoration volunteers spending about 40,000 hours began building a replica SPAD XIII in 2006; Bill Rodgers and Joe Kosek headed up this effort. The SPAD was the Allies' best fighter aircraft in World War I—pilots included Frank Luke, first air recipient of a Medal of Honor, and Eddie Rickenbacker, Medal of Honor recipient and leading US ace in World War I, with 26 enemy aircraft destroyed. The team finished work in 2014, using blueprints translated from French. All of the wood parts were constructed at the museum. The aircraft is very close to being flyable. Shown are the SPAD's frame (above) and the finished aircraft now on display (below). The World War I wooden hangar structure, also constructed by volunteers, was the first completed diorama in the current facility. (Above, courtesy of Al Hudson; below, photograph by the author.)

Lifetime member Paul Fullerton donated this Schweizer TG-3A glider in 2014. It had been in storage for years and had deteriorated. Museum volunteers are spending about 10,000 hours to restore it. Shown is work on the wing structure, which used computer-controlled machining—recreating the spar and rib assembly in one piece, saving many hours of work. Also shown is progress through 2017. Schweizer built 113 TG-3As, which were used as a trainer for World War II glider pilots on missions such as the D-Day landing. Glider pilots never got the recognition accorded bomber or fighter pilots, but they should have—each mission ended up as a controlled crash in enemy territory. Gen. James Gavin remarked that flying a glider "is a chastening experience. It gives a man religion." (Above, courtesy of Al Hudson; below, photograph by the author.)

This is a partial Consolidated B-24 fuselage that was manufactured at Willow Run, then transferred to the Royal Canadian Air Force, mated to a PB4Y tail, which was built by Consolidated and used by the Navy. The interior view of the fuselage below, taken from the bomb bay area, shows the cavity where the ball turret would have been, two openings for the waist gunners, and the rear turret gunner's station. Even though B-24s were big aircraft (about 67 feet long), with a 10-man crew, bombs, guns, oxygen tanks, and ammunition, space on a mission was at a premium. The fuselage will come to NMAT as an example of Willow Run's assembly process; riveting work is ongoing. (Both photographs by the author.)

McDonnell's F-101 Voodoos played multiple roles in the Air Force, such as a strategic fighter, bomber escort, and photo reconnaissance during the Cuban Missile Crisis and in Vietnam. Reconnaissance crews believe the RF-101C flew some of the fastest missions ever flown in combat. This Voodoo was an early acquisition; shown above is the aircraft being trucked to Michigan in 1983 from the NMUSAF. Two and a half months of work were required to disassemble the wings and remove the engines to get the aircraft ready for transport to the museum. This F-101 was used to test ejection seats—a very important project, as early ejection seats were extremely dangerous for crew members. The Voodoo is shown below in 2017; this aircraft is seen as a long-term restoration project. (Above, courtesy of Dennis Norton; below, photograph by the author.)

The Soviet-designed Antonov AN-2 Colt had a production run from 1947 to 2001, with over 18,000 produced in the Soviet Union, Poland, and China. Very rugged and versatile, the Colt was used to haul cargo and troops, and was used for civilian passenger transport. In a January 1968 incident, a North Vietnamese AN-2 was shot down by a US Huey helicopter—one of the very few instances of a fixed-wing aircraft being shot down by a helicopter. This aircraft was flown by Aeroflot out of the Soviet Union, then was in Lithuania and Sweden before making its way to the United States in the mid-1990s. After multiple ownership changes, it was found abandoned in a field in the early 2000s. The AN-2 was eventually donated to the museum, where extensive restoration work was completed. (Above, courtesy of Al Hudson; below, courtesy of Melissa Workman.)

Six

EVENTS

World War II hero Lt. Col. Richard Cole (far right) is pictured at the museum in 2009. Cole participated in the Doolittle Raid in April 1942 as Jimmy Doolittle's copilot. Each Raider received a Distinguished Flying Cross for the mission. In 2014, Congress passed legislation awarding the Raiders the Congressional Gold Medal for "outstanding heroism, valor, skill, and service to the United States in conducting the bombings of Tokyo." (Courtesy of Bruce Stoddart.)

The museum has engaged in some friendly competition with the World War II Home Front National Historical Park in Richmond, California, to have the most "Rosie the Riveters" in one place at one time. A series of events have been held in Michigan and California, with the number of participants certified. The "Rosies" dress in bandanas, work boots, dark blue work clothes, and red socks. Pictured above are four Willow Run Rosies getting ready to check in entrants at the 2014 event. Below are participants in the museum's 2016 event. The October 2017 event smashed the record: more than 3,700 Rosies were on hand. Executive director Kevin Walsh noted, "We meet women . . . from all walks of life, who trace their success back to Rosie the Riveter breaking down barriers." (Both, courtesy of Al Hudson.)

Volunteers and staff work hard, but there is nothing wrong with having some fun. This photograph shows the 2016 American Bistro Night, which had a 1940s theme. There was good food, good times, and some great music performed by the Couriers, with vocals by the Ladies for Liberty. Not many facilities offer a backdrop of a B-25 bomber for a dinner dance. (Courtesy of Al Hudson.)

The museum's natural focus is aviation, but many people interested in airplanes and aviation history are also interested in classic cars. This photograph shows a beautifully restored Ford Thunderbird, taken at the second annual Willow Run Victory Car Show: Celebrating Willow Run's Heritage in 2016. The event is lots of fun for the participants, and proceeds support the museum. (Courtesy of Al Hudson.)

A Technology, Engineering, Aviation/Aerospace, and Mathematics (TEAM) summit for girls ages 7 to 13 was hosted in October 2014. The program's vision was to help girls consider careers in fields such as technology, engineering, aviation/aerospace, and mathematics. Various speakers provided their personal insights, and several hands-on activities were available. Some attendees got to fly on private aircraft with female pilots. (Courtesy of Al Hudson.)

Bomber buffing has been an annual springtime event since 1995, giving volunteers the opportunity to get up close with the flyable aircraft. The 2012 buffing was held at the airport in Grosse Ile, Michigan, which was used for several years after the 2004 fire for flyable aircraft winter storage. Here, the *Yankee Lady* is getting a shine, and volunteers are sending a greeting ahead of a trip to the air show in Pellston, Michigan. (Courtesy of Al Hudson.)

The museum hosted NASA's Fly Me to the Moon traveling exhibit from February to May 2013 as part of the museum's ongoing efforts to reach young people. This educational exhibit featured a variety of interactive science experiments and exhibits concerning space shuttle repairs, astronomy, and a moonwalk. A replica of the Lunar Module was on hand. On February 9, former astronaut Jack Lousma participated in the opening ceremony by giving a speech and signing autographs. Lousma, born in Grand Rapids, Michigan, was a Marine officer and aviator, Skylab 3 astronaut, and space shuttle mission commander. He is a director of the Michigan Aerospace Foundation, Yankee's fundraising arm, and is shown at left below with volunteers John Yates, Linda Catalano, and Bob Catalano. (Both, courtesy of Al Hudson.)

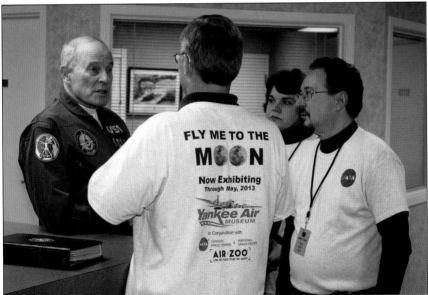

Memorial Day has featured a wide variety of programs and speakers over the years, and these events all require volunteers to make them work. This 2010 photograph shows the ramp crew, who oversee rides on the flyable aircraft. Ramp crew personnel receive specialized, ongoing training for their responsibilities. They are the first responders if there is a safety issue, assist passengers in boarding and deplaning from the rides, and provide general security for the guests and aircraft. Crew members benefit from having experience in commercial ground operations; they are outside and on their feet for long hours, in sometimes very hot weather. Events usually require various refreshments to be available, and once again, volunteers such as Darlene Imus (below) step up and provide hospitality to visitors. (Both, courtesy of Al Hudson.)

The volunteer appreciation dinner is an annual tradition. This photograph is from the 2016 event. The speaker is executive director Kevin Walsh. The museum has about 250 day-to-day volunteers, covering every aspect of operations: marketing, communications, education, security, retail, aircraft maintenance, and restoration, to name a few. After dinner, progress over the past year and future plans and challenges are discussed, and the Volunteers of the Year are recognized in each department. (Courtesy of Al Hudson.)

The museum offered its first Touch Tour for the visually impaired in March 2016. Docents led about a dozen guests on tours of museum aircraft and artifacts, allowing for a different interpretive experience compared to sighted guests. Staff received special training from the state of Michigan to ensure an informative and enjoyable experience for visitors. (Courtesy of Al Hudson.)

The 2014 Yankee Gala, an annual dinner and award event, recognized three future leaders in STEM (Science, Technology, Engineering, and Math): Zoe Jones, Anea Gaskin, and Jeremy Spink, all from local high schools. The gala theme, "Building the Future. Preserving the Past," highlights the museum's interest and emphasis on education and supporting science-related career aspirations in young people. (Courtesy of Al Hudson.)

The Vietnam Veterans of America, Plymouth Canton chapter hosted a traveling Vietnam memorial wall exhibit in 2005 at the museum. This exhibit is a replica of the Washington, DC, display honoring those who died in the conflict. The names of over 58,000 servicemen and women are engraved on the wall, allowing visitors to reflect on the sacrifices made during this difficult time in US history. (Courtesy of Dwight Koslowski.)

Seven

SPEAKERS

Lt. Col. Charles Kettles was the featured speaker in a July 2017 event. Kettles was awarded a Medal of Honor for his actions as a Huey helicopter pilot in May 1967 in Vietnam, which was presented to him in 2016 by Pres. Barack Obama. Kettles originally received a Distinguished Service Cross. A local historian began the process to upgrade the original award to a Medal of Honor. (Photograph by the author.)

Lt. Col. Alexander Jefferson served with the Tuskegee Airmen, flying on 19 missions before being shot down and captured by the Germans. Jefferson flew North American P-51 fighters and other aircraft as part of the 332nd Fighter Group, known as the "Red Tails." After the war, he became an elementary schoolteacher and cofounded the Detroit chapter of the Tuskegee Airmen. (Courtesy of Al Hudson.)

Longtime volunteer Dale Burgess spoke to a general membership meeting in 2013. Burgess was a Lockheed P-38 Lightning pilot in the Pacific, flying with Charles Lindbergh as well as America's top World War II ace, Major Richard Bong. After finishing college, Burgess worked in the civilian world and remained in the Reserves. After retiring, he volunteered for many different organizations, including the museum. (Courtesy of Al Hudson.)

Brig. Gen. Steve Ritchie spoke at the 2013 gala. Ritchie was the only US Air Force pilot ace of the Vietnam War, shooting down five North Vietnamese aircraft. At one point during his service, Ritchie flew the museum's F-4C and autographed part of the landing gear. "Duty, desire, and determination" is Ritchie's view as to how to lead one's life. (Courtesy of Al Hudson.)

Another distinguished speaker was Steve Pisanos. Born in Greece, he emigrated to the United States and began flying for the Eagle Squadron, US volunteers in the Royal Air Force before America's entry into World War II. Pisanos downed 10 German aircraft over 100 missions before mechanical problems forced him down behind enemy lines. He worked with the French resistance before being reunited with US forces. (Courtesy of Al Hudson.)

Former congressman John Dingell, a Democrat from Michigan, speaks at the 2013 Veterans Summit. Dingell was one of the last World War II veterans in the House; he held office for 59 years—the longest of anyone in that office. He was on the floor of the House as a page in December 1941 when Pres. Franklin Roosevelt declared war on Japan. (Courtesy of Al Hudson.)

Dr. John Clark had an extraordinary career as a B-17 copilot, author, and professor at the University of Michigan. His late wife, Marie Mountain Clark, was a World War II Women Airforce Service pilot, then had a distinguished musical career, including principal flute in the Ann Arbor Symphony Orchestra. Here, Clark speaks to the 30th anniversary Yankee Gala in 2011, where he and Marie were honored with the museum's Visionary Awards. (Courtesy of Al Hudson.)

Longtime Detroit TV personality Sonny Eliot spoke at the museum in 2007. Eliot was a B-24 pilot in World War II; he was shot down and spent 18 months as a prisoner of war, where he helped organize entertainment for the captured crewmen. Eliot then got into broadcasting in 1947 in metro Detroit and was featured in a wide range of roles; he was best known as a weatherman. (Courtesy of Dwight Koslowski.)

Retired Navy commander Paul Galanti speaks at a 2017 Historic Presentation Night. Galanti flew 97 missions during Vietnam, was shot down, and spent over six years as a prisoner of war. His late wife, Phyllis Galanti, was a leader of POW support causes. Galanti eloquently spoke about his experiences, including some dry humor: "There is no such thing as a bad day when you have a doorknob on the inside of a door." (Photograph by the author.)

At the 2014 gala, Visionary Awards were presented to Judith Christie (left, receiving the award on behalf of her grandfather, William Knudsen) and to Jonna Hoppes (below, accepting on behalf of her grandfather, Jimmy Doolittle). Knudsen, after holding senior positions at Ford and General Motors, was instrumental as codirector of the Office of Production Management, overseeing the conversion of US manufacturing to a wartime basis. Doolittle, one of the most famous aviators in American history, won the Medal of Honor for planning and leading the bombing attack known as the Doolittle Raid on Japan in April 1942. He also provided various advisory services relating to Willow Run and earned one of the earliest doctorates in aeronautics. He piloted the first aircraft to land at Willow Run. (Both, courtesy of Al Hudson.)

Bob Mason (right), a Huey helicopter pilot, wrote *Chickenhawk*, a critically acclaimed account of his time in Vietnam. His friend Jerry Towler also was a helicopter pilot during the war. Mason's original edition of the book used pseudonyms for some of the soldiers—for example, Towler was "Glen Resler." Mason and Towler both spoke at a May 2011 event describing some of their combat experiences, including the 1965 battle at Ia Drang valley in South Vietnam—one of the first major encounters between the US Army and North Vietnamese regular army soldiers. Helicopter pilots and crews experienced very heavy casualties in Vietnam while flying mission after mission; Mason and Towler provided first person accounts of their experiences. (Both, courtesy of Al Hudson.)

Apollo 13's Lunar Module pilot, Fred Haise, spoke at the 2015 Yankee Gala. Haise shared recollections from the Apollo 13 mission, where the astronaut's lives were saved through a series of unprecedented actions by NASA personnel and the astronauts themselves after an explosion on the spacecraft's service module. He noted that Apollo was "the greatest program of the 20th century, given the engineering that went into it." (Courtesy of Al Hudson.)

So many volunteers have contributed so much to the museum. One such individual is Norm Ellickson, who has contributed about 50,000 hours of work since 1981, including serving as the B-17's crew chief. Here, he is recognized at the 2012 Yankee Gala. Ellickson won the 2014 International Council of Air Shows Special Achievement Award for his years of work in the aviation community. (Courtesy of Al Hudson.)

Eight

THUNDER OVER MICHIGAN AIR SHOW

Thunder Over Michigan 2014 was graced by the Willow Run Rosies, seen here posing by the B-24 *Diamond Lil.* Rosie leader Alison Beatty is in the back row at center; the four women in the middle row worked at local defense plants during World War II. The Rosies provided an incalculable amount of work for the war effort; today's volunteers help keep their memory alive by spreading the message to save the Willow Run bomber plant. (Courtesy of Al Hudson.)

The first official Thunder Over Michigan was held in 2003. Previously, various aviation events were held at Willow Run when the museum participated with airport authorities. All of these events rely on volunteers—starting with 47 people in 2004, now about 700 work the event each year. Especially important volunteers are the "garbage grunts," who ensure runways are clear of debris and keep the grounds clean. It is not a glamorous job, but it is critically important. The Grunts' motto is "When everyone else has to go home, we get to stay." Coordinator Dave Steiner manages the volunteers, which is no small undertaking. Guests get to see a wide range of historic aircraft and aerial acrobatic shows, take great pictures, and enjoy a day at the airport. (Above, courtesy of the Terpstra Collection; below, courtesy of Dwight Koslowski.)

The Air Force Thunderbirds were formed in May 1953 as the Air Force's official air demonstration team, activated at Luke Air Force Base in Arizona. Maj. Dick Catledge, a training squadron commander at Luke, was named the first team leader. Over the years, the Thunderbirds have used many aircraft that have been part of Yankee: The F-84F Thunderstreak, F-105 Thunderchief, F100 Super Sabre, and the F-4 Phantom. The Thunderbirds now fly General Dynamic's F-16 Fighting Falcons; millions of people worldwide have enjoyed their shows. The Thunderbirds' first appearance at Thunder was in 2014. Shown above is some really low-level flying. Below is a group shot of the aviators and ground crew with some young fans. (Both, courtesy of Al Hudson.)

The mission of the US Navy's Blue Angels is to inspire a culture of excellence through flight demonstrations and community outreach. To support that goal, the Blue Angels have appeared at Thunder five times through 2017. Formed in 1946 at the direction of Adm. Chester Nimitz, their first commanding officer was Lt. Comdr. Roy Voris. They were called back to active duty during the Korean War, forming the core of Fighter Squadron 191 (VF-191), known as "Satan's Kittens" in 1950, on the USS *Princeton*. Precision flying—high speed, low altitude, in very tight formation—is a high-risk proposition. These pictures, from Thunder 2011, show the Angels in formation and performing aerial acrobatics in McDonnell Douglas F/A-18 Hornet aircraft. (Both, courtesy of Al Hudson.)

Thunder 2004 had a Republic P-47D Thunderbolt, *Hun Hunter XVI*, on hand. The livery of this aircraft is in honor of Lt. Col. Gil Wymond, who won a Silver Star for his actions in a P-47 in Italy, then starred in the 1947 film *Thunderbolt*. This aircraft saw service with the Brazilian Air Force before being returned to the United States. It was restored to flying status in 1999. (Courtesy of Dwight Koslowski.)

Thunder 2004 also featured a Grumman F4F-3 Wildcat. During a 1944 training mission from the deck of the USS *Wolverine*, this airplane crashed and sank in Lake Michigan. It was raised in 1991, and after years of restoration work, was certified as airworthy in 2002. Wildcats saw service with the US and British navies, as well as with the Marines in World War II. (Courtesy of Dwight Koslowski.)

Another World War II veteran at Thunder 2004 was this Consolidated PBY-5A Catalina. PBYs were used extensively in World War II for antisubmarine warfare, convoy escorts, rescue missions for downed airmen, and cargo transport. They were amphibious, able to land at sea or on land. This aircraft saw service with the US Navy and Coast Guard, was decommissioned, and then was used in Canada for aerial survey work. (Courtesy of Dwight Koslowski.)

Fifi is shown at Thunder 2012; at the time, it was the only flyable Boeing B-29 Superfortress in the world. Manufactured in Renton, Washington, in 1945, the aircraft was assigned to a training squadron before being mothballed in 1958. In 1971, the Confederate (now Commemorative) Air Force acquired this aircraft, which was named in honor of the original owner's wife, Josephine "Fifi" Agather. (Courtesy of Al Hudson.)

A North American F-100 Super Sabre arrives at Thunder 2010. This particular aircraft saw service in the Turkish Air Force, was obtained by the US Air Force, and was going to be used as a target practice drone. The drone plan changed, and the aircraft was purchased and restored by Dean Cutshall of Fort Wayne, Indiana, and a team of mechanics and restoration personnel. (Courtesy of Dwight Koslowski.)

Thunder 2010 featured a flight of two P-51 Mustangs and an F-16 Falcon. The Mustangs are part of the "Horsemen," an aerial acrobatics team that uses vintage aircraft. The Falcon was flown by Capt. Ryan Corrigan of Viper Team East Demo Team, and the Mustangs were flown by Horsemen Jim Beasley and Dan Friedkin. (Courtesy of Al Hudson.)

Witchcraft, one of the two flying B-24s in the world, was at Thunder 2010. This B-24 was built at Consolidated Aircraft's plant in Fort Worth, Texas, and was transferred to the Royal Air Force. After several changes of ownership, including the Indian Air Force, the Collings Foundation in Hudson, Massachusetts, obtained it. After five years and 97,000 hours of work, *Witchcraft* (then named *All American*) flew in 1989. (Courtesy of Al Hudson.)

In 2011, Thunder featured a Mitsubishi A6M3 Zero, flown in from the Commemorative Air Force Southern California chapter. The A6M3 was an upgraded version of the original Zeros in service at the beginning of World War II with the Japanese Navy. This Zero was recovered in New Guinea in 1991; restoration work took a number of years to complete, with the aircraft being reregistered in 1998. (Courtesy of Al Hudson.)

Also featured in 2011 was this P-51C Mustang, *Tuskegee Airmen*. This aircraft was a US-based trainer in 1945 that was acquired by the Commemorative Air Force in the 1980s and restored to flying condition. The (faintly visible) phrase "By Request" under the side window signifies that the 332nd Fighter Group, manned by Tuskegee pilots, were often specifically requested to escort bomber aircraft because of their reputation and skill. (Courtesy of Al Hudson.)

Vought F4U Corsairs were known as "Whistling Death" by the Japanese (the air intakes in the wing roots sometimes resulted in a whistling sound) and had a unique, gull-wing design. Corsairs saw service in World War II and Korea and were used by Maj. Gregory "Pappy" Boyington in VMF-214, "Black Sheep Squadron," a very famous group of Marine pilots in the South Pacific. These Corsairs were at Thunder 2011. (Courtesy of Al Hudson.)

The Douglas A-1 Skyraider is shown at Thunder 2013. Skyraiders saw service in Korea and Vietnam. The Navy used them for carrier-based strikes; Air Force usage included pilot rescue escort missions—Skyraiders would fly cover and help direct helicopters to downed airmen. The *Naked Fanny* nose art is a play on words of a base in Thailand: Nahkon Phanom. (Courtesy of Al Hudson.)

The *Spirit of Freedom* Douglas C-54E appeared at 2014 Thunder, having served with the Army Air Forces, Navy, and Marines, and participated in the Berlin Airlift. It was ultimately purchased by the Berlin Historical Airlift Foundation, which added a flying museum/memorial commemorating the airlift in the C-54's interior. In 1998, the *Spirit* flew on a European tour commemorating the airlift's 50th anniversary. (Courtesy of Al Hudson.)

This Bell P-63 Kingcobra appeared at Thunder 2014. The P-63 had an atypical design—a cannon that fired through the propeller hub, an engine behind the pilot, and cockpit access through a door, not a sliding canopy. Most saw service with the Soviet Union; there is some dispute about whether P-63s were primarily ground support or if they played a broader role for the Soviet military. (Courtesy of Al Hudson.)

Thunder 2015 attendees saw the only flyable de Havilland DH-98 Mosquito, a British World War II aircraft used as a bomber, fighter, and for reconnaissance missions. Mosquitoes were high speed and very maneuverable, built mostly of wood. This aircraft was manufactured in Canada and had multiple owners before being obtained by the Military Aviation Museum in Virginia Beach, Virginia. AVspecs of New Zealand completed the restoration over eight years. (Courtesy of Al Hudson.)

The Douglas A-26 Invader is shown at Thunder 2015. The Invader was the only US bomber to see service in World War II, Korea, and Vietnam. This particular aircraft is known as the *Silver Dragon* for the paint scheme on its nose. At the 2016 Oshkosh air show, the nose landing gear collapsed, but no one was hurt and the aircraft was restored to flying condition. (Courtesy of Al Hudson.)

The only known flyable Consolidated Privateer (Navy derivation of the B-24) in the world was at Thunder 2015. This aircraft was restored to its original Navy configuration by GossHawk Unlimited of Casa Grande, Arizona, after serving for years as an aerial tanker fighting forest fires. This Privateer had been finished in orange and white markings while flying on tanker duty for different companies through 2006 in Wyoming. (Courtesy of Al Hudson.)

Nine

THE PAST LEADS TO THE FUTURE

Dennis Norton, Museum member No. 1 and a 2018 inductee into the Michigan Aviation Hall of Fame, is an instrumental figure in bringing NMAT to life. He would quickly note he did not do it alone, but it is hard to imagine either today's museum or NMAT without him. In his view, NMAT will "let us save a critical piece of US history—the arsenal of democracy." (Courtesy of Al Hudson.)

The Willow Run bomber plant began manufacturing aircraft parts in 1941, with the first Consolidated B-24 Liberator bomber coming off the line in 1942. The original plant was 3.5 million square feet—about a mile long and a quarter mile wide. The plant was designed by Ford chief engineer Charles Sorenson, who essentially sketched it in one night on hotel stationery after visiting Consolidated's plant in San Diego, California. In the early days, the plant was known as "Will-It-Run," given the poor quality of the finished aircraft. It was a huge transition for Ford to go from automobile to aircraft assembly. In a concerted effort by all—management, workers, suppliers, and the government—quality problems were largely resolved, and a bomber an hour was soon coming off the line. (Both, courtesy of Yankee Air Museum.)

Willow Run had a 90-degree turn at the end of the production line that fed into the rollout hangar, the museum's future home. It is believed that the turn was built to keep the manufacturing facility entirely in Washtenaw County, avoiding Wayne County's higher taxes (the plant is on the county border). This photograph shows B-24s coming down the line and making the turn. (Courtesy of Yankee Air Museum.)

Henry Ford takes President Roosevelt on a tour of Willow Run in September 1942. Ford's chief engineer, Charlie Sorensen, is in the front seat. Roosevelt and Ford were bitter political enemies; it may have been a somewhat uncomfortable ride through the plant. Henry's son Edsel Ford was instrumental in getting his father to agree to plant construction. (Courtesy of Yankee Air Museum.)

Female participation in the World War II defense industry was essential; about 40 percent of the Willow Run workers were women. A B-24 had over 300,000 rivets, with over 500 variants, none of which were installed by robots. Museum visitors today who worked at the plant often remember the noise from the rivet guns and other equipment. It was extremely demanding, exhausting, and hazardous work. (Courtesy Yankee Air Museum.)

Willow Run produced 8,685 B-24 Liberator bombers—an essential part of the Allied effort in World War II. B-24s were used in all theaters of the war on bombing, transport, and anti-submarine warfare missions. According to Historian Stephen Ambrose, "It would be an exaggeration to say that the B-24 won the war for the Allies. But don't ask how they could have won the war without it." (Courtesy of Yankee Air Museum.)

After World War II, Willow Run was obtained by Kaiser-Frazer, which manufactured automobiles from 1947 to 1953; over 739,000 cars and a limited number of C-119 Flying Boxcar aircraft were made here. Henry Kaiser, a ship building magnate, entered the automobile industry after World War II, forming the Kaiser-Frazer Corporation in 1945 with Joseph Frazer. Kaiser-Frazer ran into financial difficulties, ultimately transferring auto operations to a plant in Ohio. (Courtesy of Ypsilanti Historical Society.)

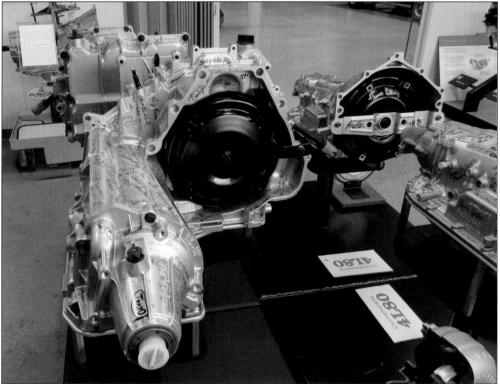

After Kaiser-Frazer's ownership, General Motors acquired Willow Run after its transmission plant in Livonia, Michigan, was destroyed by a fire. About 82 million Hydra-matic transmissions were manufactured here beginning in late 1953. This was the last transmission off the line, built in December 2010. It is now at the Ypsilanti Automotive Heritage Museum in Ypsilanti, Michigan. (Photograph by the author.)

Chairman Ray Hunter speaks at the bomber plant dedication in June 2015. The museum is in the midst of a major project to renovate the plant into a state-of-the-art museum and events facility. When complete, Yankee will be renamed the National Museum of Aviation and Technology at Historic Willow Run (NMAT). Significant construction and fundraising progress has been made, with a projected opening date in the early 2020s. (Courtesy of Al Hudson.)

Bob and Terri Lutz visited the museum in May 2017. Bob is campaign cochairman of the Save the Bomber Plant campaign—the fundraising effort for converting the plant to NMAT. Lutz has had an extraordinary career—Marine A-4 aviator, then a wide range of senior leadership positions at Ford, General Motors, and Chrysler. They are pictured in front of an A-4C. (Courtesy of Dennis Norton.)

This photograph gives a sense of the scale of the NMAT project. The Bond with the Bomber Plant open house was held in 2015. The roof and walls leaked, the floor needed new concrete, and there was no electrical, sewage lines, or water. However, the potential for a world-class facility in a historic World War II plant remains the driving force behind this effort. (Courtesy of Al Hudson.)

NMAT's construction has many unique challenges. The nearest utility lines are over 2,000 feet away from the building. Extensive excavation work is needed for utility lines and the related piping and valves for these systems. About six inches of concrete over 144,000 square feet of floor space is required. Also needed are a fire suppression system, parking lot improvements, interior build out and painting, and heating and cooling systems. (Courtesy of Kevin Perlongo.)

As part of the environmental cleanup efforts, a French drain was installed to remove excess water runoff from under the plant. RACER Trust, which works closely with the Environmental Protection Agency and the Michigan Department of Environmental Quality, is responsible for environmental remediation efforts. Significant time, money, and effort is being invested in this effort to ensure an environmentally sound result. (Courtesy of Kevin Perlongo.)

The museum's future home has a new neighbor: the American Center for Mobility (ACM) test facility, one of 10 national proving grounds for autonomous and connected vehicles in the United States. At a ground-breaking ceremony for ACM, Michigan governor Rick Snyder suggested thinking of Willow Run as an "opportunity to lead our future"—just like the original bomber plant. This photograph shows road work underway as of 2017. (Courtesy of Kevin Perlongo.)

Work quickly began on the building after finalizing the purchase with RACER. Construction efforts began in December 2014, and by winter 2015, sufficient progress had been made to move several aircraft indoors. Indoor storage is important, as Michigan's climate is not very friendly for outdoor aircraft storage. Shown here is the move-in of two of the museum's aircraft. Above is the DHC-4 Caribou, the second one off the production line. Below is a Martin RB-57A Canberra, the first of the RB-57A photo reconnaissance variant produced. The museum's RB-57A saw service in Germany and various US Air Force bases. In addition to automobiles, Kaiser-Frazer manufactured about 70 C-119 Flying Boxcars at the bomber plant in 1952 and 1953—thus, the museum's aircraft were the first in Willow Run after an over 60-year pause. (Both, courtesy of Al Hudson.)

Artist renditions of the future NMAT are shown in these two images. AECOM is the architectural firm on the project, and the senior design architect is Fred Gore. When finished, the facility can be used as an event center holding up to 1,000 people and will house all of the static aircraft, offices, classrooms, and restoration areas. After move-in, Yankee Air Museum will be under one roof for the first time since the 2004 fire. The museum will then have the added benefit of being in a facility that was a key element in the Arsenal of Democracy. Guests will thus be visiting over 80 years of industrial and manufacturing history in southeast Michigan. (Both, courtesy of Yankee Air Museum.)

About the
Yankee Air Museum

The Yankee Air Museum, founded in 1981, is a 501(c)(3) nonprofit organization, located at 47884 D Street in Belleville, Michigan.

Fast Facts

Ray Hunter, Chairman
Kevin Walsh, Executive Director
Website: www.yankeeairmuseum.org
Telephone: 734-483-4030

Smithsonian Institution affiliate

National Museum of the United States Air Force, National Naval Aviation Museum, and National Museum of the Marine Corps approved loanee

Unity in Learning Partnership: Ann Arbor Hands on Museum and Leslie Science & Nature Center

Member of the Association of Science and Technology Centers, Michigan Museums Association, International Council of Air Shows, Michigan Historical Society

Michigan Activity Pass participant

Local chambers of commerce and visitors/convention organizations member

The first member of the museum, Dennis Norton, is now the president of the museum's fundraising arm, the Michigan Aerospace Foundation, a 501(c)(3) nonprofit organization.
Website: www.michiganaerospace.org
Telephone: 734-999-8052

DISCOVER THOUSANDS OF LOCAL HISTORY BOOKS FEATURING MILLIONS OF VINTAGE IMAGES

Arcadia Publishing, the leading local history publisher in the United States, is committed to making history accessible and meaningful through publishing books that celebrate and preserve the heritage of America's people and places.

Find more books like this at
www.arcadiapublishing.com

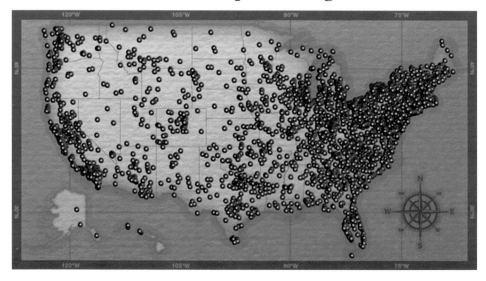

Search for your hometown history, your old stomping grounds, and even your favorite sports team.

Consistent with our mission to preserve history on a local level, this book was printed in South Carolina on American-made paper and manufactured entirely in the United States. Products carrying the accredited Forest Stewardship Council (FSC) label are printed on 100 percent FSC-certified paper.

MADE IN THE

USA